A fuss on the bus

Dad has a job on the bus. It is a big, red bus.

Miss Quinn has her piglet and her bag on her lap.

Miss Quinn has a red hat on. A bug is on her hat.

Miss Quinn hops up to get the bug off. Her bag tips.

Lemons, eggs and carrots fill the bus.

The piglet hops into the mess. Miss Quinn is upset.

14

Miss Quinn is quick to get off the bus. Dad is quick to get a mop!

Before reading

Say the sounds: c k ck j qu v w x y z zz ff ll ss

Practise blending the sounds: job Miss Quinn buzz mess carrots fill quick

High-frequency words: Dad a on it big up get off has is
Tricky words: the her to into
Vocabulary check: fuss – getting very upset about something

Story discussion: What is happening in the picture on page 8? How do you think Miss Quinn feels?

Teaching points: Check that children can read the graphemes c, j, qu, zz, ff, ll, ss. Pick one or two of these graphemes and ask children to find and read a word with each in the book. Check that children can retell the main points of the story during and after reading. Check that they can identify and read the tricky words: the, her, to, into. Discuss and read words with two syllables, e.g. piglet, carrots, upset.

After reading

Comprehension:
- Who is on the bus?
- What does the bug land on?
- What makes a mess on the bus?
- How do you think Miss Quinn feels in this story?

Fluency: Speed-read the words again from the inside front cover.